How to Hold a Crayon

● Drawing Lines or Letters

Grip the crayon between your thumb and index finger, and then support it with your middle finger.

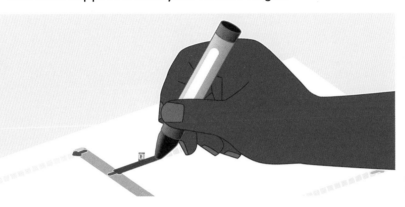

● Coloring

Grip the top of the crayon firmly between your thumb and index finger.

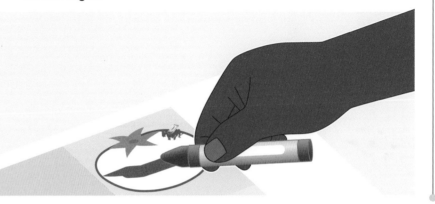

How to Hold a Pencil

● Hold the pencil at a 60-degree angle.

● Hold the pencil just above the sharpened part. Be careful not to put too much pressure on your fingers.

● Grip the pencil between your thumb and index finger, and then support it with your middle finger.

● For writing practice, use a shorter, fatter pencil, as it is easier to grip.

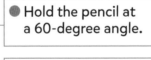
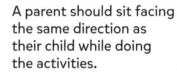

A parent should sit facing the same direction as their child while doing the activities.

Let's Hold the Crayon and Pencil Properly!

T0060090

Draw Horizontal Straight Lines

To Parents: In this activity, your child will practice drawing short horizontal lines. Because children of this age usually do not apply much pressure when writing, have them use crayons that are easy to color with.

Draw lines from  to . Place the stickers on .

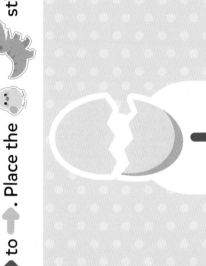

sticker

sticker

*The activities in this book are designed to be completed in landscape orientation.

Draw Vertical Straight Lines

Draw lines from ↑ to ↑ . Place the 🐝 stickers on sticker .

3

Draw Diagonal Lines

To Parents: In this activity, your child will practice drawing diagonal lines. It's okay if your child draws a longer line and goes beyond the dotted lines. When they're finished, praise your child, saying, "Well done!"

Draw lines from ⬆ to ⬆.

Draw Vertical Straight Lines

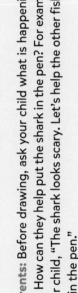

Sticker

Good job!

Draw lines from ⬆ to ⬆.

Draw Short Curved Lines

To Parents: In this activity, your child will practice drawing short curved lines. If it seems difficult, put your hand on your child's to draw. Make sure to let your child draw ears as well. Encourage conversation by asking why the animals are smiling.

 Good job! Sticker

Draw lines from to ⬆.

Draw Short Curved Lines

To Parents: Say to your child, "These children are sound asleep." Have your child draw the short curved lines of the children's closed eyes and hair, one by one. Encourage conversation by asking your child about their bedtime routine.

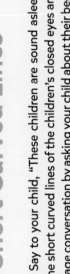

Draw lines from ⬆ to ⬆.

Draw Arched Lines

To Parents: In this activity, your child will practice drawing a series of consecutive arcs. Make sure your child stops at the end of each arc before moving on to the next.

Draw lines from ➡ to ➡. Place the sticker on sticker.

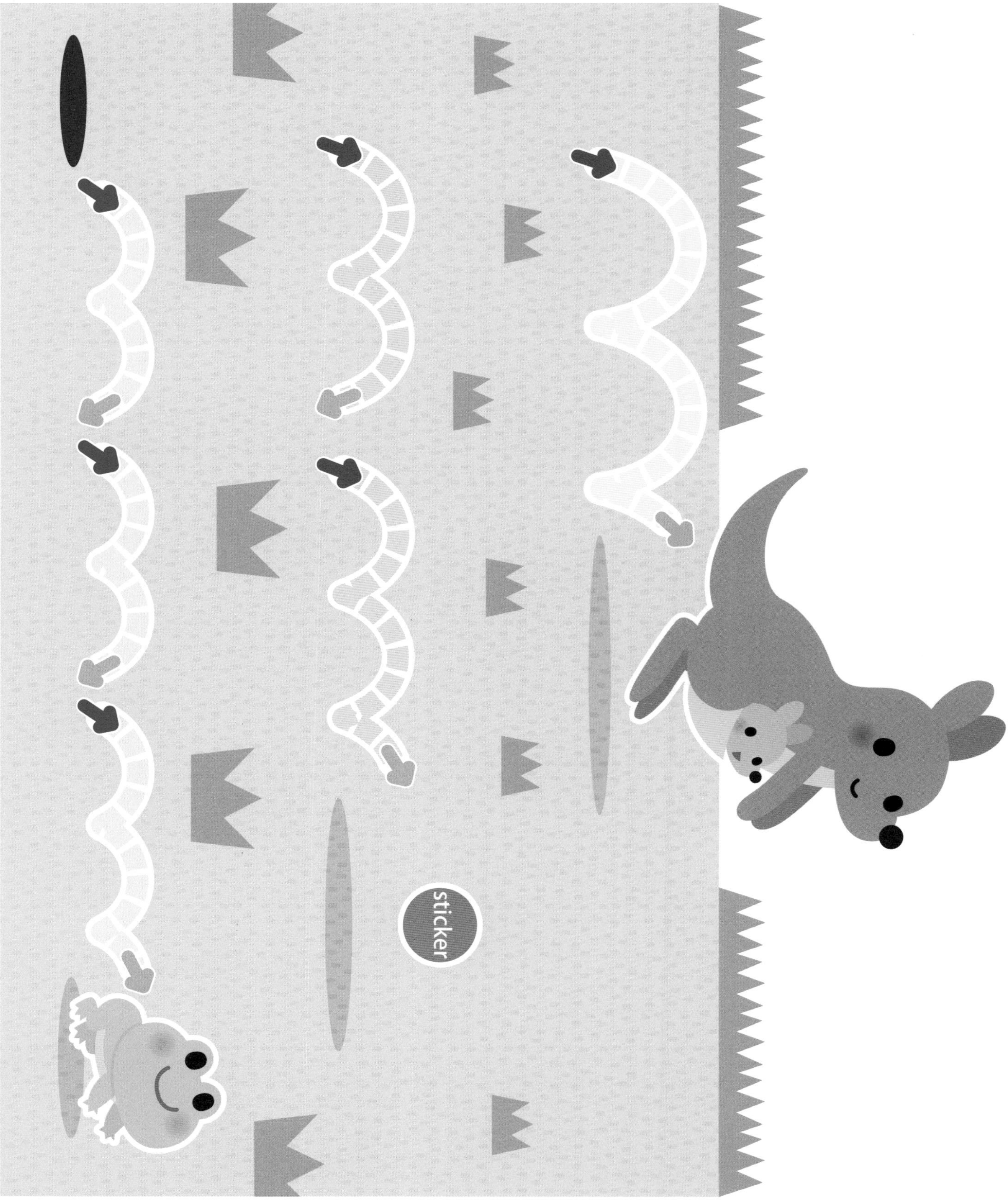

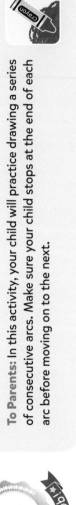

Draw Arched Lines

Draw lines from ↑ to ↑. Then fold along the dotted lines for a surprise!

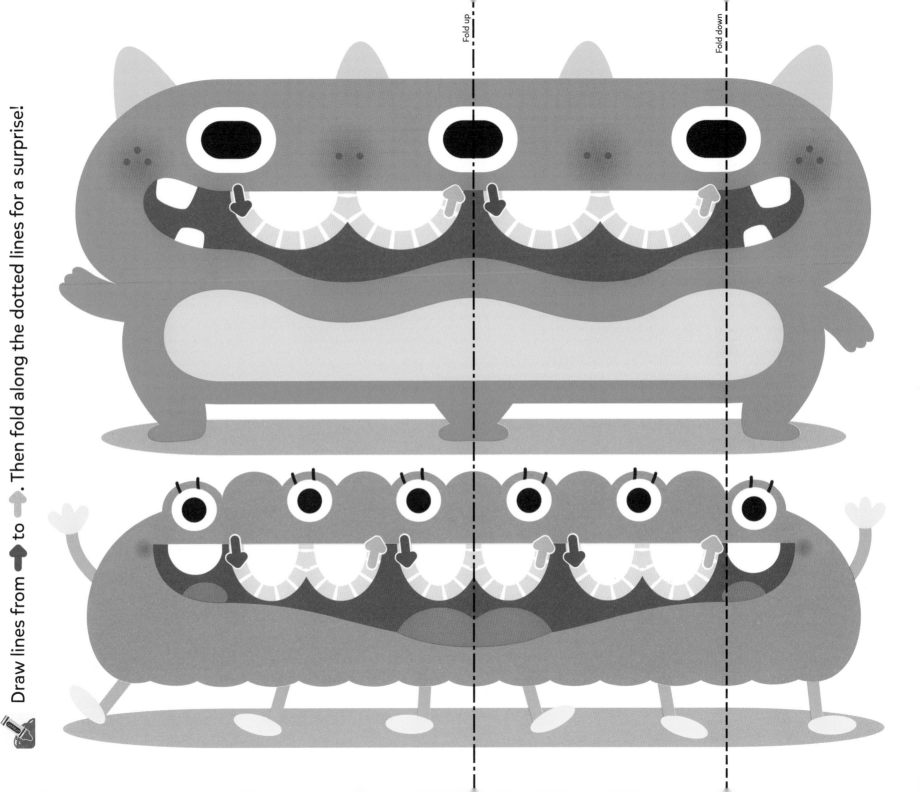

Fold up

Fold down

Good job!

Sticker

9

Draw Wavy Lines

To Parents: In this activity, your child will practice drawing wavy lines. If that seems difficult, encourage your child to first slowly trace the lines with their finger. After applying the stickers, ask your child, "What's the name of this car?"

Draw lines from to . Place the  stickers on sticker.

Draw Wavy Lines

Good job!

Sticker

Draw lines from ⬆ to ⬆. Then fold along the dotted lines for a surprise!

Fold up

Fold down

11

Draw Circles

To Parents: In this activity, your child will practice drawing circles. It's okay if your child doesn't trace well. If this seems difficult, put your hand on your child's to help them draw. When they're done drawing, encourage them to count the circles.

Draw lines from ⬆ to ⬆. Then color the bodies of the caterpillars.

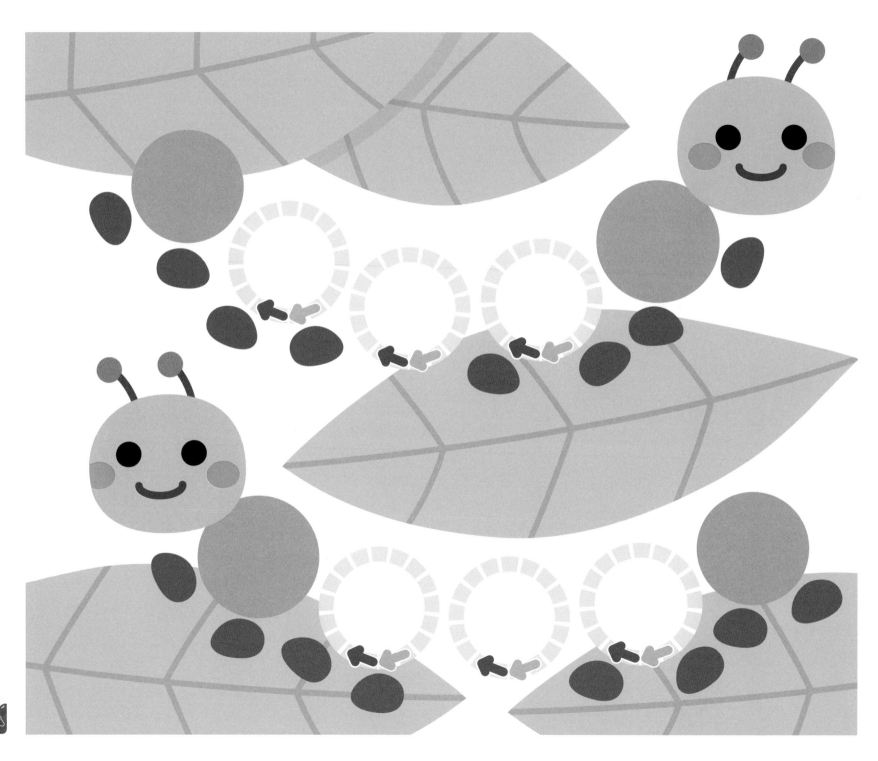

Draw Circles

To Parents: Draw circles while saying the names of the objects: flower, bee, ant, and ladybug. This helps your child build vocabulary while drawing. Praise your child when they're done with the activity, even if they cannot make an exact circle.

Sticker

Good job!

Draw lines from ⬆ to ⬆. Then color the flowers.

Draw Jagged Lines

To Parents: This activity focuses on drawing jagged lines. Encourage your child to stop at each bend before changing direction.

Sticker

Good job!

Draw lines from ⬆ to ⬆.

Draw Zigzags

To Parents: This activity focuses on drawing consecutive zigzags. This provides basic practice for writing the alphabet.

Draw lines from ⬆ to ⬆.

Draw Spirals

Good job!

Sticker

Using the same color crayons as in the picture, draw spirals from ↑ to ↑.
Then draw tails on the cat and pig as well!

Draw Spirals

To Parents: Draw together with your child while saying, "These noodles go around and around." When parents join in the activity, children become more motivated!

Using the same color crayons as in the picture, draw spirals from ⬆ to ⬆. Then draw some noodles!

Draw Dots

To Parents: Learning to draw dots is similar to learning to draw short vertical lines. It's okay if some dots are a little longer than others.

Good job!

Sticker

Let's draw seeds on the watermelon and strawberries.

Water the Flowers

To Parents: In this activity, it is okay for your child to draw lines instead of dots. It's more important that they feel they watered the flowers by themselves. When they're done, say to your child, "Well done! The flowers are watered!"

Draw dots. Place the  stickers on .

Sticker

Sticker

In the Desert

Good job!

Sticker

Draw lines from ⬆ to ⬆.

20

Play on the Playground Bars

To Parents: This activity focuses on drawing longer straight lines. Encourage your child to draw a continuous line without stopping.

Draw lines from ⬆ to ⬆.

Play on the Swings

To Parents: This activity focuses on drawing longer straight lines. Encourage your child to practice drawing lines, not only from top to bottom, but also from bottom to top.

Draw lines from ↑ to ↑. Place the stickers on .

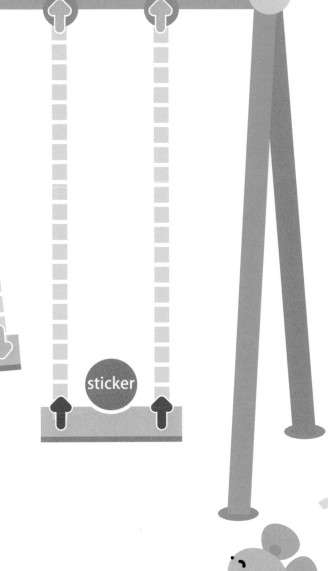

Play on the Slides

To Parents: In this activity, your child will practice drawing diagonal lines. Offer your child encouragement by saying, "Help the animals slide down."

 Draw lines from ⬆ to ⬆.

Clean the Room

To Parents: Ask your child, "What sound does a vacuum cleaner make?" While they're drawing the lines, say, "Vroom! Vroom!"

Help the lion clean the room. Draw lines from to . Place the ★ stickers on  .

Go to the Bathroom

Good job!

Sticker

Help each animal get to the bathroom. Draw lines from ⬆ to ⬆.

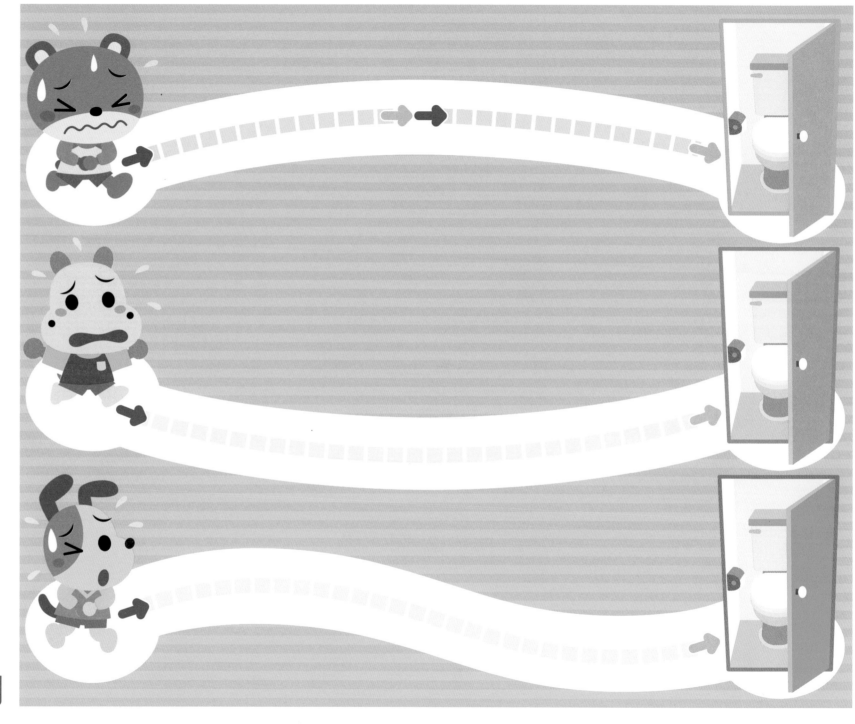

26

Go to the Bathroom

Help each animal get to the bathroom. Draw lines from ↑ to ↑.

Wash Our Hands

To Parents: This activity focuses on drawing successive arches from different directions. If this seems difficult, when your child stops drawing halfway through, put your hand on your child's to draw the lines together.

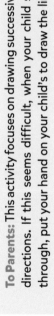 Draw lines from ⬆ to ⬆ to make soap bubbles.

Dry Our Hands

Draw lines from ↑ to ↑ to make hand towels.

Play with Balls

To Parents: In this activity, your child will practice drawing consecutive arches. Encourage your child to draw each arch in one stroke. When they're done, say, "The soccer ball is bouncing!"

Draw a line from  to  to show how each ball bounces. Place the stickers on sticker.

30

sticker

sticker

sticker

Good job!

Draw Clouds in the Sky

To Parents: This activity allows children to focus on drawing half of each cloud at a time. Let your child draw clouds in the open space, too.

Draw lines from ↑ to ↑ to make clouds.

Good job!

Sticker

Draw Crab Legs

To Parents: In this activity, your child will practice drawing bent lines. Guide your child to stop at the bend in each leg before changing direction.

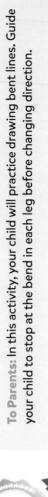

Draw lines from ⬆ to ⬆ to make legs for the crab.

32

Draw Alligator Teeth

To Parents: As your child draws the lines, develop vocabulary by saying, "Zigzag! Zigzag!" If drawing the zigzags seems difficult, ask them to first try drawing the alligator's top teeth.

Draw lines from ⬆ to ⬆ to make alligator teeth.

33

Draw the Castle

To Parents: In this activity, your child will practice drawing part of a square. Encourage your child to work slowly, and to pause at each corner before making the turn.

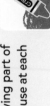

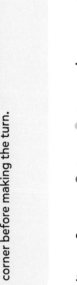

Good job!

Sticker

Draw lines from ⬆ to ⬆ to make a castle. Place the 👑 sticker on sticker.

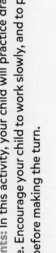

sticker

Play with Bubbles

Draw lines from ↑ to ↑ to make bubbles.

Sticker

Good job!

crayon

35

Draw Snails

Draw the line from ⬆ to ⬆ to make each snail's shell.

Play with Butterflies

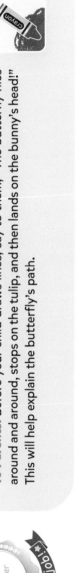
Good job!
Sticker

Where does the butterfly fly? Draw a line from  to .

37

Find and Trace 1, 2, 3

To Parents: Guide your child's hand to help them trace the numbers. Then encourage them to trace alone. After they draw the numbers, ask your child, "How many elephants are there?"

Find 1, 2, and 3 in the picture. Then trace the numbers from ⬆ to ⬆.

Good job!

Sticker

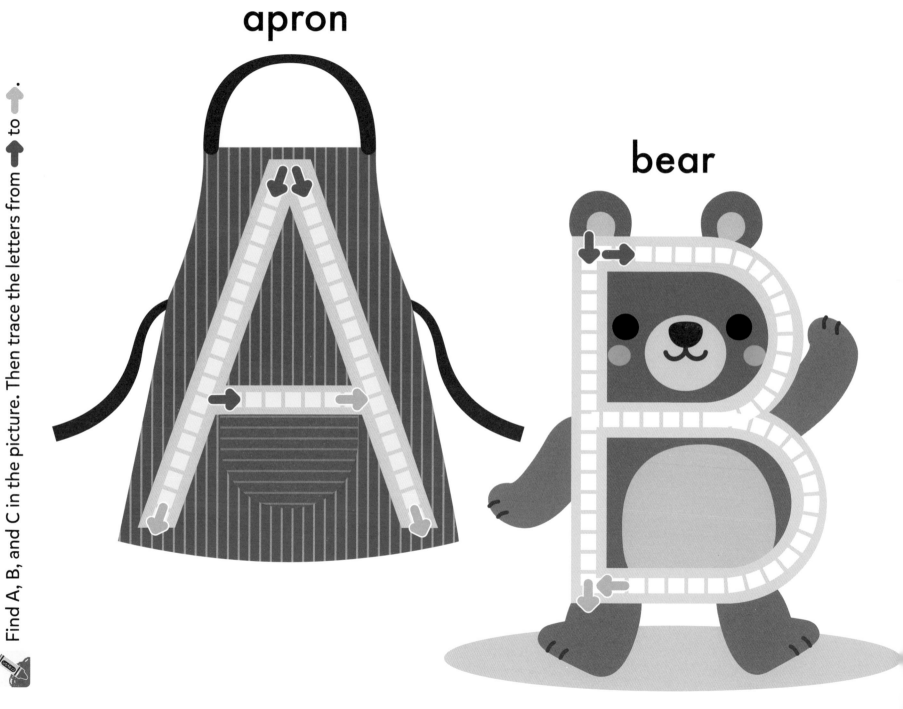

Find and Trace A, B, C

To Parents: Encourage your child to trace each letter with their finger, following the arrows. If this seems difficult, try holding your child's finger to help them trace the letter. When they're done, say, "A is for apron. B is for bear. C is for cup and cow."

Find A, B, and C in the picture. Then trace the letters from ⬆ to ⬆.

apron

bear

Good job!

Sticker

cup

cow

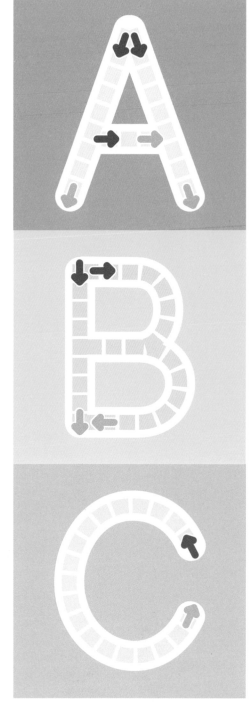

Find the Matching Vehicles

To Parents: For the next few activities dotted lines are not used. Let your child find matching vehicles and draw lines connecting them by themselves.

Draw a line to connect the matching vehicles in each box.

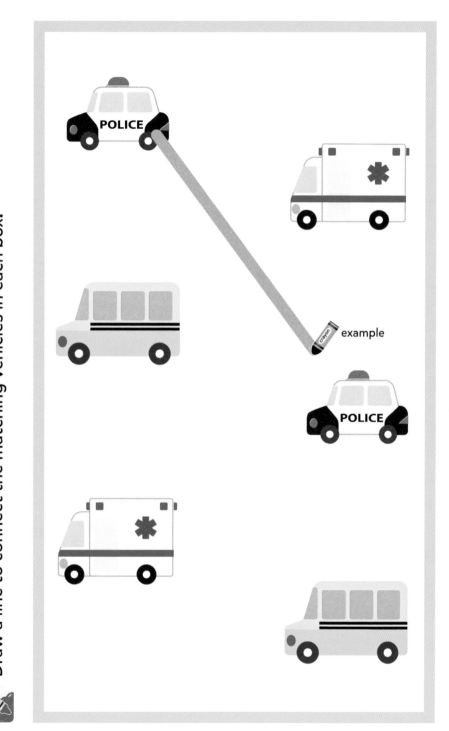

example

example

Good job!

Sticker

Find the Matching Toys

To Parents: Ask your child to begin by finding the matching objects, and then drawing a line to connect them. It's okay if your child's lines aren't perfect in connecting the pairs. It's more important that the lines are going in the right direction.

Sticker

Good job!

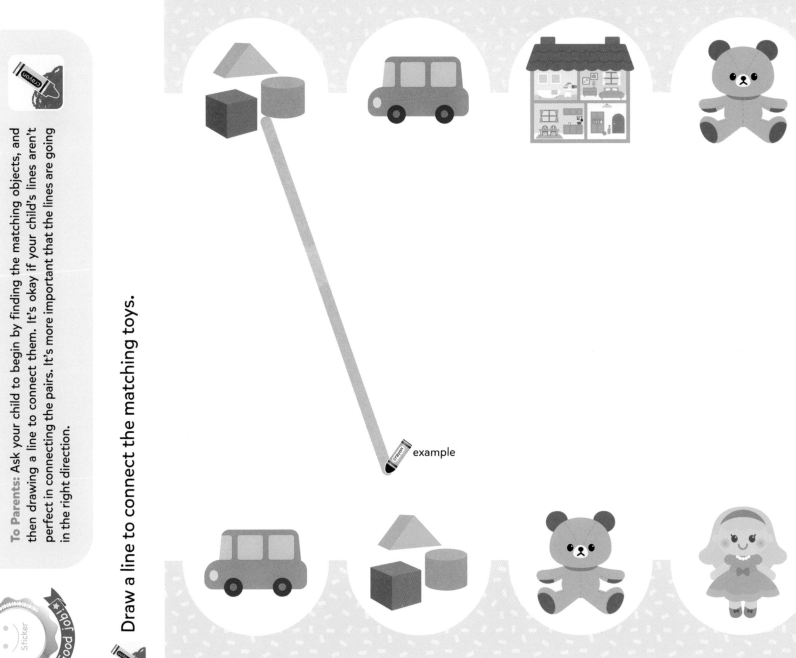

example

Draw a line to connect the matching toys.

Find the Matching Clothes

To Parents: Some children may not want to cross over the lines they have drawn. If your child is avoiding crossing lines, tell them that it's okay to overlap!

Draw a line to connect the matching clothes.

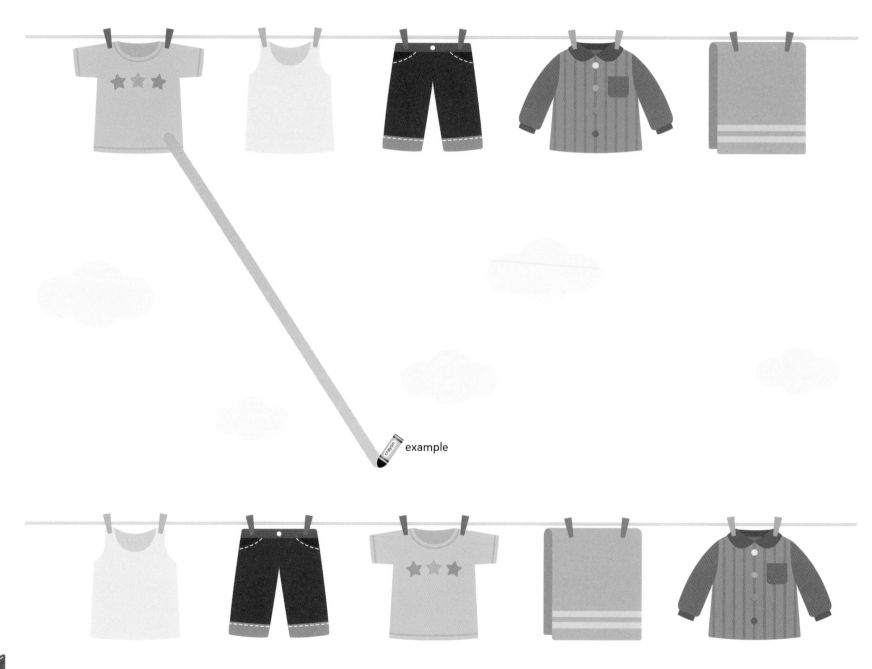

example

Good job!

Sticker

Find the Matching Animals

Draw a line to connect the matching animals.

example

Sticker

Good job!

Go Through the Maze

Sticker

Good job!

Help the chick find its mom. Draw a line from ⬆ to ⬆.

example

Go Through the Maze

Help the cow find the farmer. Draw a line from ⬆ to ⬆.

Sticker

Good job!

Go Through the Maze

To Parents: Tell your child to stop drawing when they need to change direction, then start again. When arriving at the destination, let your child say, "I'm here to deliver the pizza."

Help the boy deliver a pizza by scooter. Draw a line from ⬆ to .

Go Through the Maze

Good job!

Sticker

Help the fire truck drive to the building that's on fire. Draw a line from ⬆ to ⬆.

Find and Trace the Shapes

Find the shapes in the picture. Then trace the shapes from ⬆ to ⬆.

Find and Trace the Shapes

Find the shapes in the pictures. Then trace the shapes from ↑ to ↑.

Draw a Turtle

To Parents: In this activity, children will practice drawing lines without using guidelines. Encourage your child to continue drawing around the turtle without going outside the white path.

Help finish the turtle's shell. Draw a line from ⬆ to ⬆.

Draw an Airplane

To Parents: The airplane below uses straight and curved lines. It's okay if your child takes a break and puts down the crayon. But encourage them to also try drawing continuously.

Help finish the airplane. Draw a line from ⬆ to ⬆.

Sticker

Good job!

55

Draw a Tulip

To Parents: If it's difficult for your child to draw one continuous stroke, ask them to first trace the line with their finger. Then ask them to draw the line.

Sticker

Good job!

Help finish the tulip. Draw a line from ⬆ to ⬆.

Draw a Dress

To Parents: Because this activity includes one continuous, long line, it's okay for your child to stop once and then start again.

Help finish the dress. Draw a line from ⬆ to ⬆.

Draw Cookies

To Parents: This activity is a review of all the activities your child has done in the book. Encourage your child to choose a different color to draw each line!

Let's make cookies. Draw lines from ⬆ to ⬆.

Good job!

Sticker

Draw a Pig's Face

To Parents: Ask your child, "Why is the pig crying?" When your child is done drawing the lines, encourage them to trace the ears and nose as well.

Let's draw a pig's crying face. Draw lines from ⬆ to ⬆ .

Good job!

Sticker

Draw a Hamburger

To Parents: This activity reviews drawing straight and curved lines. As your child draws, say, "Hamburger, fries, and juice."

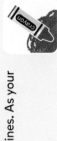

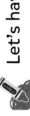

Let's have lunch. Draw lines from ⬆ to ⬆. Draw dots on the hamburger.

Connect the Dots

To Parents: To begin, count the numbers 1 to 5 aloud with your child. Then ask them to trace from dot to dot with their finger as you count.

Connect the dots in order: 1→2→3→4→5. Color the ice cream any color you choose!

Sticker

Good job!

example

Connect the Dots

To Parents: If doing the dot-to-dot activity seems difficult for your child, help them by putting your hand over your child's and drawing the lines together.

Connect the dots in order: 1→2→3→4→5. Color the rabbit any color you choose!

Good job!

Sticker

Connect the Dots

To Parents: After counting from 1 to 10, ask your child to draw the lines. If counting is still too difficult, ask your child to connect the lines by following the arrows.

Sticker

Good Job!

Connect the dots in order from 1 to 10. Color the fruit any color you choose!

Connect the Dots

To Parents: When your child is done connecting the dots, ask, "What kind of vehicle is it? Who is in there?"

Connect the dots in order from 1 to 10. Color the vehicle any color you choose!

crayon

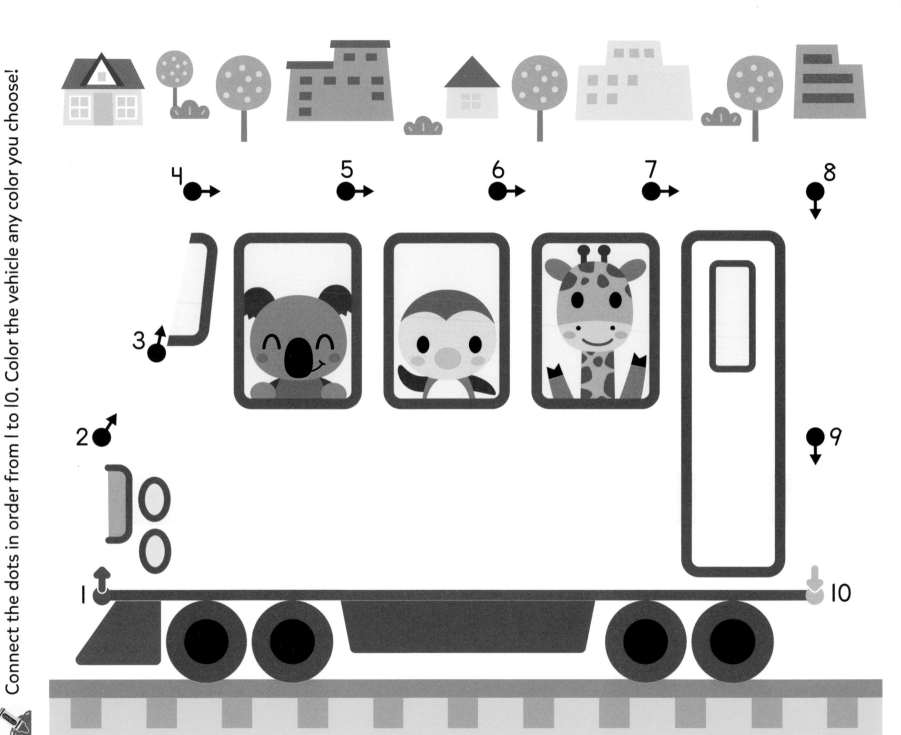

Good job!

Sticker

64

WIPE-CLEAN ACTIVITY BOARD

Trace the lines with your favorite colors.

Use water-based markers on this side of the board. When your child is finished drawing, erase the board with a damp cloth or a tissue.

Trace lines with your finger to connect the matching things.